The Discovery Adventure Club

by Deb Ingino

Illustrations by Joelle Felyce Geisler

The Discovery Adventure Club
by Deb Ingino
Illustrations by Joelle Felyce Geisler

Dedicated to:
Children everywhere,
those young and those young at heart.

100% of Proceeds from The Discovery Adventure Club book
go to Prodigal House. Prodigal House is a program of LIYFC, providing
emergency and short-term residential housing for teenage boys ages
12-16. Programs are designed to address behavioral issues.
The short-term environment, change and interaction with Prodigal
House staff gives each boy the opportunity to find their purpose in life.

For more information visit: www.prodigalhouse.com

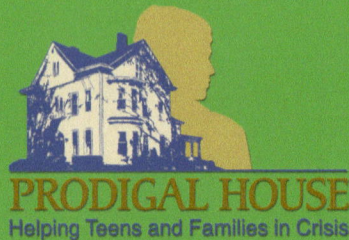

PRODIGAL HOUSE
Helping Teens and Families in Crisis

Verto Press, New York ©2010. All Rights Reserved.
ISBN # 978-0-9823557-4-9
www.mywiredstyle.com

VERTOPRESS
NEW YORK

Once upon a time, there were four friends who called themselves the Discovery Adventure Club.

The four friends were Daniel, Isabelle, Sasha and Caden. Sasha had been very sad because she lost her pet ferret, Stripes. So her friends planned an adventure in Isabelle's backyard to cheer her up.

As the friends arrived, Isabelle was so excited to see them that she screamed when she saw them coming toward her gate, "Hi everyone, I'm so excited you are here!"

Then Isabelle ran and knocked poor Sasha down onto the grass with her great big hug. Isabelle was so excited. She loved having fun with her friends and Sasha liked having such a good friend in Isabelle.

"Oops" frowned Isabelle. "Sometimes my hugs are bigger than I am."

"That's okay" Sasha giggled, "I like big hugs!"

Daniel looked down and saw a really big backpack by Caden's feet.

Daniel said, "You must be really hungry Caden. That is a big lunch bag."

Caden looked down and replied, "My lunch is in there, but so is the map for our adventure and three books on different kinds of trees and birds."

Daniel said, "Caden, we can't carry that around all day long. Why don't you take your lunch out of that bag and let's start our fun?"

Caden really liked having his books and map with him.
At home he even has his bookcase next to his bed.

Caden told Daniel, "I'll carry it.
It's not very heavy, and I have
my map so we can start
our adventure."

Daniel said, "I will take the map and lead the way."
Daniel liked being in charge. At home he is even in
charge of his goldfish, Joe. He likes leading his friends.

So The Discovery Adventure Club friends
began their adventure.

As they walked along, they saw a pretty bird flapping its wings so fast that you almost could not see them move.
"I wonder what kind of a bird it is?" blurted out Isabelle.
"Shhh" Daniel hushed, "Izzy, you don't want to scare him away, do you?"

"Awww, that birdie is so cute" said Sasha, "I wish I could take it home." Just then Caden found a picture of the bird in his book and sounded out the name. "It looks like it's a hummm-ing-bird."

"That's right!" Daniel said. "It's a humming-bird alright!"

Once the hummingbird flew away
the four friends began to walk further
under the trees. They came to a cool spot
with lots of shade.
Daniel said, "Here, this is our lunch spot."
Isabelle agreed, "Hooray, I love this spot!
Sasha come sit next to me!"

Sasha was concerned, "Are you sure this spot is safe? That tree is really tall."

Sasha can sometimes be a little afraid to be in a new place.

"Don't worry" said Caden, "This tree is strong and it has leaves on all of its branches. My books say that if trees have leaves on their branches in summer they are safe."

He continued, "This one has a lot of leaves."

The four friends enjoyed a picnic under the big tree. Isabelle told them many fun stories and everyone was laughing. The friends were happy to see Sasha laughing even though she had been so sad about losing Stripes.

After they were full from lunch Daniel said, "Time to go. Our adventure is not over."

Daniel said,
"Let's go over by the pond to see if there are any frogs."
So the four friends walked over to the pond and Daniel
stepped into the pond to get a closer look.

"I don't see any frogs" said Daniel.
Isabelle agreed, "I really like frogs.
I like to hear them say ribit, ribit."
"I hope we see a cute little animal for me to hold."
Sasha sighed, "I so miss Stripes."

"I like how high frogs can jump" said Daniel, "They are the best jumpers."
Caden replied, "Daniel, frogs aren't the best jumpers. I read that Kangaroos are the best jumpers." Daniel didn't like being corrected, "I knew that Caden, I meant here in the pond."

The four friends rested by the pond until Caden noticed, "Look, the sun is starting to go down and we have to go soon before it gets dark."

Daniel agreed, "Caden is right, it is time for us to go."

As the Discovery Adventure Club left the pond they passed by Isabelle's backyard garden and saw two little eyes peeking out from the bush.
"Oh how cute" Isabelle yelled as she raced over to the bush.
"Wait Izzy!" cautioned Caden, "we should make sure that animal is safe; let me look in my book."
Daniel said, "I think I've seen those eyes before."

Just then Sasha rushed over to the bush
and screamed with joy, "Stripes, I found you!
How did you get all the way to Isabelle's backyard?
Were you on an adventure too?"

Sasha picked up Stripes and gave him a big hug,
just like the one Isabelle gave her when they started
their adventure. Daniel and Isabelle smiled
when they saw how happy Sasha was to find Stripes.

The four friends ran inside
announcing the good news
to Isabelle's Mom.
She then called Sasha's Mom
and told her how the
children found Stripes.
Sasha's Mom came right
over and found them all
in Isabelle's yard.
As Sasha saw her
mom, she exclaimed,
"MOM! Look I found Stripes!"

Sasha's mom was thrilled and said, "Oh Sasha, you must be
so happy!" She continued, "It was so nice of your friends
to plan this adventure hoping to cheer you up and having
found Stripes, the adventure couldn't be any better!"

As Sasha's Mom left to take Stripes back home, Isabelle said "Sasha I'm so glad you found Stripes, this really did turn out to be a great adventure!"

Sasha replied, "Izzy, it was the best adventure ever. I am lucky to have you, Daniel and Caden as friends. I'm lucky to have Stripes back too."

Caden added,
"I liked that we saw the hummingbird. Their wings go so fast."

"It was fun" said Daniel, "I'm glad Isabelle told us stories that made us laugh and I'm happy that Sasha found Stripes.

Caden, your books helped us with the hummingbird and I'm glad I was leading us through the adventure. I knew it would be fun."

The Discovery Adventure Club decided they were a very good team together. Each of them made the adventure something special.

They made plans to meet again and go on another adventure.

Which of The Discovery Adventure Club friends are you most like?

Daniel, who likes to make decisions and be in charge?

Isabelle, who likes to tell stories and sing songs to her friends?

Sasha, who is a loving and caring friend to everyone?

Caden, who makes sure he has the right information?

Your DISCovery Adventure

As you read across, find the statement or word that BEST describes you when you are at school or at home. Circle only one word or phrase on each line going across.

I want things done	The way I say	With everyone having fun	Without being mean	Without mistakes
I like to be	In Charge	Cheerful	Caring	Right
A Sign on my Room might say	"Go Away"	"Let's play"	"Quiet Please"	"Clean, Don't Touch"
Rules are	Not for me	Not fun	For our Safety	So things are Fair
I work best	Alone	With others	Quietly	With the facts
Others say I am	Bossy	Fun	Nice	Smart
I Like	Adventure	Being friendly	Getting along	Knowing details
I will	Convince others my way	Talk a lot with others	Get everyone to be nice	Notice mistakes
Sometimes I am	Bossy	Show off	Fearful	Fussy
In a group I want to be	The Leader	Making others happy	Helping everyone	The Planner
When someone yells	It doesn't really bother me	I feel they don't like me	Feel upset and want to do good	I worry I did something wrong
I often	Make decisions by myself	Am part of a group	Do what others like	Do what I'm told
I want to be	The Boss	Having fun	Helping people	Correct
I don't like	To be told what to do	Doing the same things	Sudden Changes	Making Mistakes
Playing team games	I only want the best players	I like to Talk and goof around	I see those that are left out	I watch what others do
I get upset when others	Take things of mine	Leave me out	Aren't nice to each other	Tell me I'm wrong
Totals of Each Row	D	I	S	C

Now that you have picked one statement in each line going across, in each column going up and down count how many phrases you have circled and in the box at the bottom write the total for that column.

DISCover Your Personality Wiring!

My Name is:_____

My Scores were: (from the previous page place your scores here)

D= _____
Determined/Decisive
Daniel

I= _____
Influencing/Inspirational
Isabelle

S= _____
Steadfast/Sensative
Sasha

C= _____
Conscientious/Careful
Caden

MY Highest Score was Letter: _____ So I am Most Like: _____

One thing I do Best is: _____

I enjoy: _____

A fun adventure I have been on was: _____

_____

_____

_____

_____

_____

_____

_____

_____

_____

_____

If your highest score was a "D" you are a determined person. You don't give up easily and you know what you want, like to be the leader and try very hard to win.

Below put a check next to all the statements that are true about you.

____ I am always busy
____ I focus on things I like to do
____ I am a very hard worker
____ I need to be more patient waiting for things
____ I like to make choices and decisions quickly
____ I don't want to talk about things, I just want to do it
____ I make up my mind and stick to it
____ I am daring and adventurous
____ I ask and ask for something until I get it
____ I like to get things done
____ I need to be more aware of other people's feelings
____ I like to do things myself
____ I need to learn how to be a better loser
____ I like to win no matter what
____ I want to be in charge
____ I like to set rules for games
____ I am confident about what I am doing
____ I need to be a better listener
____ I don't like to be told no
____ I get angry when I cannot make things do what I want
____ I can be impatient
____ I am not easily discouraged
____ I am willing to speak out about things
____ I am courageous
____ I don't like it when I'm told what to do
____ I need to pay attention to details better

If your highest score was an "I" you are an influencing person. You really love and enjoy people. You are happy to be involved in social activities.

Below check all the statements that are true about you.

____ I am always happy to see my friends
____ I focus on things that will be fun
____ I love getting together for exciting events
____ I need to be more organized
____ I like talking and sharing
____ I need to be more focused on projects
____ I like to be playful and use my imagination
____ I am popular with my friends
____ I like to be the center of attention
____ I like to be cheerful and make people feel happy
____ I am friendly and impulsive
____ I can be too loud
____ I need to learn that routine is important
____ I like it when I am told how good I am
____ I don't like to be excluded from activities
____ I like to express my thoughts
____ I don't like being alone
____ I need to be a better listener
____ I sometimes do things I shouldn't so that others will like me
____ I get upset when I can't talk
____ I can be impatient
____ I am can be easily discouraged
____ I like to make the best of a situation
____ I like to daydream
____ I am good at doing things while others watch or listen
____ I need to learn to finish chores quicker

If your highest score was an "S" you are a steadfast person.
You are very kind, patient and friendly.
You are respectful and enjoy helping others.

Below put a check next to all the statements that are true about you.

____ I am very loyal to my friends
____ I am patient with people
____ I am a good listener
____ I don't like to argue with people
____ I like to be helpful to my family and friends
____ I feel as if someone doesn't like me if they yell at me
____ I will follow what the group is doing to keep people happy
____ I am sometimes afraid of new places
____ I am very easy going and don't like to fight
____ I need to learn to speak up for myself better
____ I am very aware of someone's hurt feelings
____ I don't like it when people take my things
____ I get hurt feelings pretty easy
____ I like it when things are safe and familiar
____ I will watch what's going on before I get involved
____ I like to play games I already know
____ I am sometimes unsure of new people and stay quiet
____ I am kind to animals and people
____ I am happy when other's tell me they liked what I did
____ I get angry when someone is being bossy or mean
____ I can have a hard time chosing things
____ I am shy
____ I am unsure if people like me
____ I don't like to give my opinion because people might not like it
____ I like to share as long as I get everything back
____ I like to be a supportive friend

If your highest score was a "C" you are an conscientious person. You really enjoy projects. You enjoy solving problems and knowing how to do things.

Below check to all the statements that are true about you.

____ I am always organized
____ I focus on details of things of interest to you
____ I love getting the right information
____ I like to be the one with the answers
____ I am annoyed with people who don't follow rules
____ I need to be more willing to listen to others understanding
____ I like to know what is expected of me
____ I like to ask questions
____ I am cautious
____ I get excited about details and technical things
____ I am critical of others that don't know the right facts
____ I can be too quiet
____ I like to work alone
____ I like it when I'm given reasons
____ I don't like to be wrong
____ I work slowly so I get it right
____ I don't like to be pressured to work quickly
____ I need to share my feelings more when I am hurt or happy
____ I sometimes go to be alone to avoid an argument
____ I like to be in a clean room and have my stuff organized
____ I am well behaved
____ I am respectful of adults
____ I like to play games according to the rules
____ I enjoy doing research and finding out information
____ I like to be on time for things
____ I need be more daring

If your child is a "D"

Their Greatest Needs are:
- Control, Seen as Competent, Admired

To Motivate them:
- Create opportunities for them to be in charge
- Encourage them to help you make decisions

They are annoyed by:
- People who are weak
- People who are indecisive
- others in charge

Sweet Spot Statements:
"I like that you are very confident"
"I like that you set your mind on things and go after it"
"I like that you are committed and decisive"

If your child is an "I"

Their Greatest Needs are:
- Fun, Excitement, Approval, Encouragement

To Motivate them:
- Recognize their good behavior
- Give them an opportunity to express their thoughts
- Give them the opportunity for social activities

They are annoyed by:
- Boredom
- Routine
- Being Ignored
- Demands of organization

Sweet Spot Statements:
"I like that you are fun to be with"
"I like that you are a friendly person"
"I like your enthusiasm... it's contagious"

For More information on Seminars, Webinars, or to host one in your area, go to: www.MyWiredStyle.com

If your child is an "S"

Their Greatest Needs are:
- Peace, Stability, Appreciation

To Motivate them:
- Create a close relationship
- Emphasize your need for their help and give them an additional boost of confidence assuring them they have what it takes to succeed.
- Thank them for their helpfulness

They are annoyed by:
- Intimidation
- Disloyalty
- Unrest, malice, injustice
- Insincerity
- Prideful people
- Conflicts

Sweet Spot Statements:
"I like that you are a caring person"
"I like that you get along with others"
"I like that you are compassionate"

If your child is a "C"

Their Greatest Needs are:
- Perfection, Sensitivity, Continual reassurance

To Motivate them:
- Explain reasons for a desired action
- Allow questions and suggestions
- Give them an opportunity to research and analyze/process directions
- Praise their hard work and focus

They are annoyed by:
- Inaccuracy
- Incompetence
- Disorganization
- Overly simplified explanations

Sweet Spot Statements:
"I like how you always try your best"
"I like that you like to be organized"
"I like that you listen to what others say and feel"

For More information on Seminars, Webinars, or to host one in your area, go to: www.MyWiredStyle.com

About the Author

Deb Ingino is President of My Wired Style, a company dedicated to helping individuals discover and nurture their strengths. Deb has creatively used DISC assessments for the past twenty years in businesses and organizations in more than 14 countries. During this work, Deb witnessed that sustained success comes to those who learn and lean into their natural strengths. That really is the key, learn your weaknesses and neutralize them, learn your strengths and maximize them.

Deb believes that we are each uniquely wired with strengths, gifts and abilities to build a successful future, if we lean into our strengths. It is true for us and for our children.

Through workshops in schools, churches, and parent groups as well as convenient online webinars, My Wired Style's program helps parents to discover their own wiring, their children's wiring and provides strategies to help shepherd children into maximizing their strengths while enjoying a more connected relationship in the 'sweet spot' of life.

Deb currently lives in New York with her amazing SC wired husband and daughter who make their family DISC Style complete.

To bring this workshop to your group contact:
Info@MyWiredStyle.com or Call (631) 880-2292
www.MyWiredStyle.com

my wired style
Success is not learned. It's discovered and nurtured.

www.ingramcontent.com/pod-product-compliance
Lightning Source LLC
Chambersburg PA
CBHW041428090426
42741CB00002B/79